Of Llamas and Piranhas

Valerie Volk

Of Llamas and Piranhas

Of Llamas and Piranhas
ISBN 978 1 76041 382 8
Copyright © text Valerie Volk 2017
Front cover photo © montgomerygilchrist
Back cover photo © Nicholas Fernandez

First published 2017 by
GINNINDERRA PRESS
PO Box 3461 Port Adelaide 5015 Australia
www.ginninderrapress.com.au

Contents

Foreword	7
Preamble	11
Trip planning	12
En route – flexitime	14
Chile	17
Mercado Central	18
Plaza de Armas	20
The streets of Valparaiso	22
The Pre-Columbian Arts Museum	24
Argentina	27
Cementerio de la Recoleta	28
Floralis Generica	30
El Ateneo Grand Splendid	32
Takes two…	34
Brazil	37
Cristo Redentor	38
Interlude	40
In the favelas	42
At the Iguassu Falls	44
End of day	46
In the bird park	48
Peru	51
Saturday with horses	52
In the Sacred Valley	54
In the square at Ollantaytambo	56
Machu Picchu	58
Another world	60
Nature walk in Inkaterra	62

Thoughts in Cusco's Cathedral	64
On the train	66
At the floating islands	68
Moving on	70
In the jungle	72
On the river	74
The comfort of the familiar	76
Piranha fishing in the Amazon	78
Of llamas and piranhas	80

Ecuador — 83
- In the iguana park — 84
- Walking with tortoises: Galápagos — 86
- Life with birds — 88
- On Espanola Island — 90
- At El Rancho Manzanella — 92

Transit — 95
- Homeward bound — 96
- Endings — 98

Foreword

Valerie Volk has an eye for the fine detail. The quirky insight is something her poet's eye latches on to and the result is poetry that is dazzling in its attention to the complexities of human nature and of nature itself. *Of Llamas and Piranhas* is a fine example. This book is a smorgasbord of images and insights from a trip to Latin America. In 'Plaza de Armas', she is in Santiago, Chile, viewing the city's central square:

> Imposing, grand
> surrounded by the testimony
> of passing years and conquerors.

But the grandeur leaves her cold. It is not the Incan Empire and its wealth and splendour, or the conquistadors bringing 'domination and control', or the

> Cathedrals, statues, palaces
> of government and justice
> custodians of culture over centuries

that she sees in the Plaza de Armas, but the dispossessed Mapuche, 'Tribe whose land this was' before any of the invaders arrived, that she identifies with. She sees a statue the Mapuche made:

> A half head
> simple, primitive
> appearing amputated

and she feels a kind of kinship with those vanished people. It is the 'modern buses crammed with tourists' that she disdains;

even though she is a tourist herself, she seems them as rapacious and plunderers.

In 'The Streets of Valparaiso', she gazes on the 'toy town houses' clinging to the hills, colourfully painted so that the sailors could see their homes 'from far away'. These walls had once expressed dissent during the Pinochet regime and are now covered in murals and street art.

> In Valparaiso walls aren't walls
> and houses aren't just buildings.

They are so vividly described they almost seem alive and the poet states that they are indeed alive: an expression of the beliefs and values of the inhabitants.

A visit to the Pre-Columbian Arts Museum has the poet musing that, 'Perhaps Columbus has a lot to answer for…' Once again, it is the art of so-called 'primitive' people, this time the Maya, that centres her:

> I'm moved to see a small clay figurine
> a Mayan woman from three thousand years ago
> her arm protectively around an aged figure.

A powerful reminder of the 'human values' that sustain our species, and in a flash forward from the Mayan era she thinks about train trips today and people giving up their seats for older travellers.

Wandering the Cementerio de la Recoleta is like a walk along the tree-lined avenues of a city of the dead, where statesmen, generals and doctors lie – 'leaders of the land' – but the final democracy of death has claimed them. Even Evita 'has joined her ancestors' after 'her brief and meteoric life'. But beyond the end of every tree-lined avenue lies the city of the living with 'skyscrapers and apartment blocks' to remind the poet that, to paraphrase, in the midst of death we are in life.

There are so many beautiful poems in this collection but my favourite is 'Interlude', which begins,

> And still she walks
> that girl from Ipanema,
> hair swinging lightly in the breeze.

This poem captures perfectly the bitter sweet melancholy of the song, where the observer watches the beautiful Girl from Ipanema, but 'she looks straight ahead, not at me'. The place where she walked is now a tourist attraction, Garota de Ipanema, and strolling minstrels 'bring her back in song'. But there is someone the poet cannot bring back.

> One who loved this song
> but never had the chance
> to listen here where it was born.

Volk imagines him strolling on the foreshore with the Girl from Ipanema, singing the song as once he had sung it for the poet.

To read these poems is to be transported in imagination to a beautiful, complex land in which great beauty and great violence have always existed side by side. Volk delves into these complexities and uses them to craft fine poetry that lingers long after the book is closed.

Antonia Hildebrand

Preamble

Trip planning

There is a moment,
some time before departure,
when panic strikes.

I flounder in a fog
of unpreparedness.
Thoughts of passports, visas,
vaccinations, foreign currency
scurry through my mind.

So much to do: cancel papers;
notify the bank; prepay bills
lest they incur late fees.
Money changing to investigate,
neighbours to alert,
house and garden care to organise,
itineraries for family
so that emergencies can find us.

And then a packing list –
what will the weather be,
what sort of clothing will I need?
What can be crammed
into the quite draconian allowance
that airlines will permit?

Sometimes I wonder
if It's all worthwhile…

But then a frisson of excitement:
suddenly you know
soon you will be boarding.
The plane will rise
and all cares drop away
with the receding ground.
Your trip has started!

En route – flexitime

It's odd indeed
when travelling east
to find our certainties obscured.
Disoriented.
Judgement clouded.
It's more than just
prescribed adjustment of our watches.
Something more basic.
We find how flawed
our sense of time becomes.

Disconcerting.
We fly towards the rising sun –
suddenly our sense of self
in time and space is gone.
It's Monday noon we leave…
but then the disappearing day
relinquishes its hold
and we are plunged in night
that races through appointed hours
(how speedy Phoebus' chariot)
until, as swiftly as it went,
the sun appears once more.

But ah… We find that time has shifted.
By sleight of hand magicians might well envy
we have returned into the previous day;
it's ours to live again.

A bonus, yes. How often
have I yearned for just this chance,
to live again an earlier day,
recapture joys of old. Or to repair
hurts that I've caused, redress
what damage I have done.

But this contrivance of the calendar
does not provide such chances.
It offers us instead new lands
to travel, new adventures
which beckon us to start.

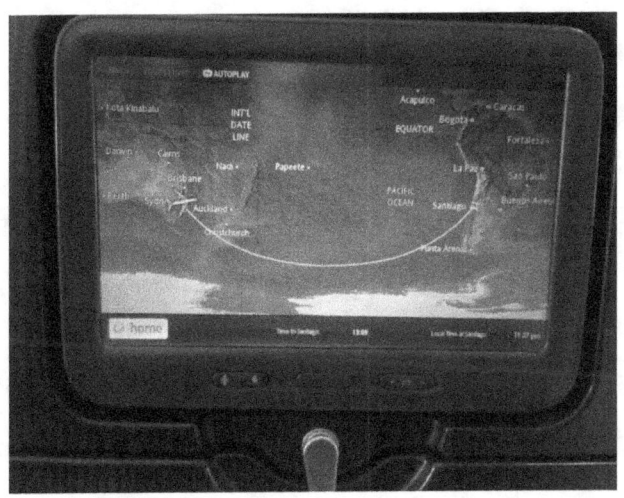

Chile

Mercado Central

Fish Market, where we stand bemused
by all those restaurants,
waiters vying for our patronage.
Beyond them on the outskirts
a small café, Mares de Chile,
its owner beaming at the door,
negotiating language barriers
to help us understand a Spanish menu.
Bare tables and no fuss –
But ah, the food!
Ceviche, from Madre in the tiny kitchen,
a taste that lingers long
with smiling chat and dictionary
to help us understand.

I'm glad we bypassed
all those central restaurants.
Who needs white tablecloths
and dinner jacket waiters
or soft red glow from shaded lamps?
Here we have a simple celebration
of good food!

Plaza de Armas

This city's central square –
imposing, grand –
surrounded by the testimony
of passing years and conquerors.
Cathedral, statues, palaces
of government and justice,
custodians of culture over centuries.

We hear the tales of Incan empire,
of wealth and splendour
and how conquistadors' invasion
brought Spanish domination and control.

But these were newcomers…
What of the simple folk before?
For all the grandeur of these sights
there's one that catches at my heart.
A massive statue, grey huge block,
a half head.
Simple, primitive.
Appearing amputated.
Mapuche.
Tribe whose land this was
before sun-worshipping Incas,
before the armoured Spaniards,
before our new invasion –
modern buses crammed with tourists
as rapacious as any who have plundered
in former centuries.

The streets of Valparaiso

Clinging to steep hills,
precariously, I feel,
these toy town houses,
crammed together,
seem products of a child's paintbox,
pictures just for our delight.

So colourful,
these brilliant dots and splashes,
while down below
the sparkling blue
of Valparaiso Bay glints
and glimmers in the bright sunshine.

Painted so returning sailors
could spot their homes
from far away, we're told.

Today those walls
give different messages.
Long used to register dissent
against the Pinochet regime,
now vibrant with street art –
murals to amuse, provoke
and even edify.

In Valparaiso walls aren't walls
and houses aren't just buildings.
They are alive – they have brought
back to life this town,
deservedly World Heritage.

The Pre-Columbian Arts Museum

There are defining moments in world history.
Columbus – and the modern world begins.
Too easy to forget
that when the Spaniards came,
lured by gold and conquest,
there was already a whole way of life
with centuries of art and culture
in lands that they usurped.
We stand before glass cases, gazing awed
at hewn stone figures, pottery bowls,
the few remaining golden figurines
that have survived the Spanish melting down.
Perhaps Columbus has a lot to answer for…

But here we find some triggers to remind us
that through the ages some things still endure.
I'm moved to see a small clay figurine,
a Mayan woman from three thousand years ago,
her arm protectively around an aged figure.
Mujer y ancien we read.
Thoughts fly to crowded Metro trips today
where with an automatic care for ageing
so many people rise to give us seats.
A care that makes us realise
though eras come and go
we can preserve the human values
which make our race worthwhile.

Argentina

Cementerio de la Recoleta

Here is another city;
its tree-lined avenues
and formal monuments
are tributes not to life
but death.

This is La Recoleta,
the City of the Dead,
who lie in mausoleums
that tower over passers-by
and dwarf us into recognition
of temporality
and our mortality.

Winds sigh through trees.
Whispering ghosts in family tombs
recall the days that they have known.
In bronze, in stone, in marble,
adorned with columns, friezes,
flanked by poignant weeping angels,
these monuments to death
guard generals, doctors, statesmen,
leaders of the land. Evita too
has joined her ancestors.
Those who bring her tributes
of daily flowers can only mourn
her brief and meteoric life.

We wander down the streets of this sad city,
indeed a City of the Dead.

But then look upwards, further see,
beyond the end of every street
skyscrapers and apartment blocks,
reminders that beyond these walls
a living city waits us,
and elsewhere life goes on.

Floralis Generica

So beautiful, this flower.
True concept of a modern age.
Stainless steel and aluminium
Its six huge petals,
twenty metres high,
rear towards the brooding sky.

Like simple sunflowers of past years
it too relies upon the sun
as source of life and light.
Its petals open, close,
according to the movement
of that master of the universe.
In dark of night it's dormant,
but rebirth comes each morning.

Said Catalano, architect,
whose gift it was to his sad city,
The name tells everything:
Generica.
It was to be a synthesis of all the flowers,
its aim rekindling of new hope each day.
As petals open, life begins again.

Our tour guide adds her own interpretation,
'He wanted it to give us hope.
A time of desperation, economy in tatters,
a population in despair.
He wanted us to see it, and believe
that each new day rebirth is possible.
So as the six huge silver petals open,
we too can gaze towards the sun
and feel once more return of hope.'

So Buenos Aires takes new heart
from this symbolic flower,
and every postcard features
Floralis generica.

El Ateneo Grand Splendid

Well, with a name like that,
our expectations had been roused
for something quite magnificent.

This bookshop, which reviewers call
'second most beautiful in all the world'
leaves visitors bemused.
A former theatre, then cinema,
it breathes the glamour of its former life.

Its theatre boxes now are quiet nooks
and readers flock to tiered balconies.
The sweeping circle of its lights
bedazzles eager shoppers; it draws
to magic other worlds.

Still today there come a million visitors
each year, just as it once invited
those earlier crowds who also sought escape
from humdrum life of everyday.

How could one not love reading
in such an atmosphere?

But there's a question in my mind:
if this is second in the rank,
who possibly would be the first,
'most beautiful bookshop in the world'?

Takes two…

In childhood I had heard that song,
beloved of the fifties,
Takes two to tango,
Two to tango,
Two to really get the feeling of romance…
but never then imagined
that one day I would stand
with fellow tourists,
apprehensive, nervous,
watching with some envy
that most evocative of dances,
Argentina's 'dance of love'.

In perfect synchronicity
the dancers swayed and swooped,
gliding gracefully across the floor,
then came to sculptured rest
poised in each other's arms.

Until that moment came
when we, the novice learners,
took tentative first steps
into this tango world.
Let's do the dance of love.

Like love, it can be beautiful.
Like love, one starts this new adventure
graceless, awkward, learning
how to be together, to move
in harmony, to lead, to follow
as the music tells us.
Like love, it needs us to become a pair
for, as that old song says,
Takes two to tango, two to tango,
do the dance of love.

Brazil

Cristo Redentor

High above this city broods
Brazil's most famous landmark.

Iconic, really. Rio de Janeiro
is home to this,
one of the seven man-made marvels
of the modern world.

We climb Mount Corvocado
the easy way – by train, but then,
with conscious virtue,
set off the last two hundred steps,
with shaming effort struggling up
the final flights. (The road to God
was never meant to be an easy path…)

But there the statue, almost forty metres,
looms high above the crowds.
Looks past the curious hundreds,
insatiable their cameras,
and, far beyond these puny creatures,
beyond the seven million people in this city,
he stretches out his arms above the land
and to the far horizon of this mighty bay.

So, overall, Christ broods, his arms
spread out in their eternal gesture
of embrace.

Ironic though, perhaps symbolic,
that each three years, the figure
must be cleaned, sandblasted.
The small mosaics that have dressed
the soapstone centre are repaired,
replaced – for time wreaks damage
in more ways than one.
And Christ, like those of us who come,
requires at frequent intervals,
a cleansing from the hazards
of the modern world.

Interlude

And still she walks,
that girl from Ipanema,
hair swinging lightly in the breeze,
hips swaying as they swayed
when Jobim and Morales
captured her in music
that the whole world knows.

Famous, that place, Garota de Ipanema,
today draws tourists
with memories on cafe walls;
two strolling minstrels
bring her back in song.
While I return in thought
to one who loved this song
but never had the chance
to listen here where it was born.
I see his spirit with her,
strolling on the foreshore sands
and singing, as he did so often,
for me, as well as her,
'The girl from Ipanema…'

In the *favelas*

'Slum tourism'
sneered a moralising friend.

I thought of this
as our small group
trekked through the alleys,
climbed interminable steep small stairs,
gazed curiously at faces
that stared back indifferently.

Their world, ruled by drug lords,
crime bosses, poverty and need…
How do these people of Rocinha,
see us, the dilettante tourists,
stepping carefully in broken alleys?
Don't wear your rings or watches!
Leave your wallets back at the hotel!
Cautiously, we pick our way,
cameras snapping at the sight
of tangled wires for stolen power,
of deep canals that take
the sewage to the sea,
of grinding cycles of a poverty
that no one can escape.

And we who walk among them,
do we have the right to drive away,
return to luxury hotels,
download our photos
for display to friends back home,
while shaking heads in wonder
that anyone can live like this?

My friend was right, for we have been,
to our eternal shame,
'Slum tourists!'

At the Iguassu Falls

Our tour group stands in wonder,
drenched by far-flung spray,
mesmerised by what we see.
For sheets of water
cascading, creaming,
rolling, roiling
spread out before us,
everywhere.

Awesome, we say,
but know the word's inadequate
to capture such magnificence.
This is a sight to make us feel
man's insignificance – for here
we find unbridled, unconfined,
untamed, untameable,
the power of nature's might,
exploding, as it has for centuries,
before man's eyes first gazed on it
in similar wonder to our own.

End of day

The log fire crackles in the grate.
Outside, darkness falls.
A different darkness, this.
Around the lodge, rain forest,
dense, foreboding, once more
looms through gathering night.
It has regained its place.
We hear of years of devastation
when coffee crops usurped the land
until, exhausted, it would yield no more.

Defeated, man accepted this reality,
and now the forest, once more
dense, foreboding, looms outside.
Tourists tread silently
their way to Iguassu Falls,
unnerved by the encroaching trees,
then, awed by that immensity of water,
return to welcome warmth.

In the bird park

Cacophony of sounds
as brilliant plumaged birds
now wheel and swoop,
delighting camera snapping tourists –
these more like hungry vultures
than the voracious birds.

We close our eyes and listen,
hear the jungle sounds
of birds who now find freedom ends
in mesh and wire that keeps them
here for our delight.
So every blaze of colour,
each toucan and macaw,
lives here confined –
but also safe from predators.
Is safety worth such sacrifice?

Peru

Saturday with horses

In Lima,
at the Hacienda Mamacona,
high-stepping horses trotted
with delicate precision. Beautiful.
The gauchos scarcely seemed
to touch the reins. They were
at one, each horse and rider,
as they wheeled and turned
before us where we sat,
murmuring in admiration.
Each delicate manoeuvre
brought a burst of clapping
not acknowledged by either
man or beast.

How sad that when it came
to our own turn to ride,
I mounted so ungracefully,
hoisted clumsily by helpful hands,
then circumnavigated the red earth
that formed the exhibition ring
uneasily.
But they were gracious
as they helped me clamber down.
'*Bueno*,' said one.
I knew he lied, but was
so grateful for the lie.

In the Sacred Valley

Deftly, she dangles llama wool
into the cast-iron pot.
The dye's already there.
'All natural, leaves and flowers,'
the guide assures us earnestly.
This is the way, even before the Incas came,
it always has been done.

The brightly clad girl pulls the wool aloft
with a magician's flourish
and beams as watching tourists clap
to see the vivid colours.
We move, directed, on to where
the spinning, weaving processes
are shown. Traditional, just like
their costumes and the big flat hats.

It's all exotic, and we stand entranced.
'Where did you learn these patterns?'
asks one man. Our guide translates,
and we are told it is a secret skill,
taught by their grandmothers.
That fits this ancient Incan Sacred Valley.

Impressive, but the modern ways
have infiltrated even here.
Our final destination? No avoiding
the mandatory stop, post demonstration,
where goods are spread for sale
and suddenly the costumed girls
have learned impressive sales-type English
and hard-sell techniques.

In the square at Ollantaytambo

Her bright dark eyes
had sized me up
quite shrewdly.
She knew a soft touch
as she held her hand
towards me.
'You want photo?'
Truth to tell, I did.
Her wizened face
beneath that bonnet hat;
bold vivid stripes of colour,
a costume every postcard
from Peru has captured.

'They will want money,'
we'd been warned by guides.
I had resisted others,
but this one had me hooked.

I took the photo, handed over
the required small coin,
but wondered why she shook her fist
at me, as I walked off.

Felt badly when a later check
revealed to me that
all those coins I'd hoarded
were in fact from Argentina,
not Peru at all.

Machu Picchu

Impossible to capture in mere words
wonders such as this. Almost
a preparation: the train that brought
the eager crowds through Sacred Valley,
the bus that mounted high
and higher, rounding hairpin bends
up into stark soaring peaks
that seemed like jagged sentinels
to guard this holy place.

But then the sight itself
of massive granite blocks, a city built
with blood and sweat and tears,
to last six hundred years,
this Incan sacred citadel.

We gaze across the valley
at temples, palaces and aqueducts
that show us still the mastery
of this past race.
The terraced agriculture…

I see it as it was:
crops from such fertile ground,
enough to feed this city
in the wilderness. But still today
there is a crop upon these terraces,
as mixed as any from past years.
Close your eyes and see
ancient Incan workers busy with
potatoes, melons, avocados,
life sustaining for their city.

Then open to a different view:
along those crowded terraces
a crop as varied: tourists, English,
French and Japanese,
Australians and Americans.
so different, so diverse,
on these same terraces.

Or just another facet of the world;
economies that change with passing time?
So Machu Picchu still sustains
her people in a different way.

Another world

At Machu Picchu
stone terraces astound.
So intricate, so perfect,
rock on rock
with seamless joins.
No mortar binding here
but just the craftsman's eye
to bring two stones together
in perfect fit.
We marvel at their skill.
A world now gone.

Today the llamas graze on terraces
just as their forebears did
six hundred years ago.
Does their race memory
still hold a trace
of ancient Inca masters?

Nature walk in Inkaterra

Along the Orchid Walk,
a feature of this ecological retreat,
Joseph stops us to explain
the wonders of these plants.
We learn about the phallic stamens
and how this process operates
to fertilise the females; see
pregnant wombs swelling
with new life.

But I am moved more by the story
of that Incan princess who loved
a commoner, a warrior, and wept
her life away when hostile father
exiled him to far-off wars.
The spirit world was merciful
and changed her to a flower –
Waqanki, loveliest of orchids.
They yielded to her lover's anguish,
on return, and granted him his plea.
So he became the humming bird
that sips perpetually from her lips,
in mankind's longest kiss.

Perhaps a gentler end than
Shakespeare gave to his ill-fated pair –
though Romeo and Juliet
live on a different way.
Yet neither pair of lovers
had the chance to propagate
like orchids.

Thoughts in Cusco's Cathedral

Ubiquitous, the guinea pigs of South America.
These days we see them differently.
No more the fluffy pets for children,
or toys beneath the Christmas tree.
For now we know they are a staple food,
skinned and roasting on the spits
of every street café.

A different role, indeed!
Brought home dramatically when,
shown Cusco's answer to da Vinci,
Zapata's picture of the famed Last Supper,
our eyes are drawn at once to food
upon that table. There it sits in splendour,
the dish for special feasting,
roasted guinea pig.

A sacrilege? No, no, our guide is clear.
This is exactly how conquistadors
and priests had brought together
the old religion that they found
and melded Incan life and ancient worship
absorbed into their own invading faith.

An ecumenical approach we might employ today?

On the train

Aptly named, this Andean Explorer.
No bullet train
hurtling through the countryside.
This train is diesel; its slow plume
of black smoke hangs beside us
as we round the river's curves.

Out of industrial Cuzco;
soon we are climbing, climbing,
ever higher in the Andes.

Beside us flows the Sacred River,
cutting deep gorges with fast streams.
We leave behind the corn crops,
neatly stooked in harvest, or in
adobe bordered plots, for now
we've reached the grassy plains
of the Andean highlands.
All around us stand like sentinels
the snow-capped Andes peaks,
guardians of this land.
Roaming herds of llamas and alpacas
set cameras snapping;
where there's cropping, it's no longer
the ubiquitous corn, but wheat.

The Cuzco dancers and musicians
entertain us in the Observation Car,
and then it's halfway point, we hear,
in this ten-hour Andean exploration.
The highest point we reach, La Raya,
at fourteen thousand feet, is our only stop.

Ten minutes, and we step with infinite care
down to the ground, gasping in the thin cold air,
where a small market waits. Colourful Mamas
all eager and importunate, hard to resist,
especially with their babies on their backs.
And such alpaca ware! Their own produce.

The day moves on through lunch,
a silver service gourmet meal,
a contrast all too clear as we observe
the tiny settlements, grey clay brick
or mud adobe, and wave to smiling people
in the fields. Or towns, where train tracks
are the central street, and carriages can
barely scrape through market stalls.
Sometimes a larger town;
like Juliaca, a motor building centre –
eye-catching university for motor trades
a startling modern contrast to the infinity
of small scrap metal stalls our train
threads through.

Outside the sun is setting, and the dancers,
now from Puno, show us that the end is near.
In darkness we pull in to Puno station, where
the air is icy in Peruvian night,
but rings of light surround our destination:
Lake Titicata waits. But what a day
it's been and, though cocooned within this shell,
we have indeed been on an Andean exploration.

At the floating islands

We'd read about these islands,
man-made, constructed out of reeds,
a total way of life for people
who have lived here since before Christ's time.
Yet, as we cruise among them,
still they surprise us. We visit Uros,
where to step ashore into so alien a life,
to meet and be shown into homes
by smiling Mamas, is entry to another world.

In brilliant sunshine, attentively we sit,
to watch their demonstration of the crafts
that are their daily life – and business.
(Wall hangings, dolls, mats – all for sale…)
'Where are the men?' we ask. We're told that
fishing is their work, as it has always been.
This culture has survived the centuries;
it has resisted all invasions, Incan, Spanish,
– can it withstand a modern world?
For on these small reed huts, where warmth
dictates the sharing of a family bed, and
Mama cooks outside as she has always done,
we note the solar panels on the roofs, and see
each hut is well equipped with a small TV set.

What will their future be?

Moving on

A travel day ahead,
which made it even harder
to sit at dawn and watch
the sun, a brilliant golden ball,
burst splendidly beyond
Lake Titicaca's distant shores.

The reed beds, floating
in a glassy mirrored sea
with all reflections gilded
like a fabled Incan temple,
seemed insubstantial
in the glorious dawn.

But then we saw the first few boats
set out among these islands:
6 a.m.; a new day starting.
A timely warning that for us too
day's routines were pressing,
and soon we'd be en route
towards the Amazon.

In the jungle

We tread with care –
although our guide ahead
has cleared the path
and wields a reassuring big machete.

But know we're right to treat
this expedition cautiously,
when we observe the anaconda,
coiled and deadly, on the track
before it slithers into undergrowth.
Or watch the boa raise his head,
scent the air with a malevolent eye,
then rearrange its deadly spirals,
poised to strike.

Our guides display to us
the poisoned spines of towering trees,
enormous spiders, ominous red backs
of sharp-nosed frogs, flesh-eating ants.
This is no place to tread too lightly!

But also note, and take to heart,
the lesson as, with care, our guide
replaces every creature just where
it was found, anxious to preserve
this jungle life as it is meant to be.

On the river

'Macaws!' says Luis Carlos.
'We call them love birds.
They mate for life, and when one dies
the other swiftly follows.'

I am besieged by old familiar guilt.
How could it be, that I,
who loved you with intensity,
with passion,
near to fifty years,
have now transformed my life,
to live and love again?

Our small skiff threads its ways
through jungle waterways
along this mighty river.

On either side encroaching jungle
looms towards us in the post-dawn hush.
The motor stilled, our guide points to
the owl-eyed monkeys near asleep,
a sloth improbably at rest high in the trees,
while squirrel monkeys scamper for the day.
A flash of blue, kingfisher darts,
and kookaburra comments take us
briefly home. The jungle's full of danger,
menaces, but glimpses of such beauty!

A sheaf of berries blazing red – but red's for danger,
and these, says Luis Carlos, will kill
not only man and beast, but birds
and insects too. Only one fish,
the Puka, can feed upon these berries
when they drop. So symbiosis once again
is underscored, as when the Tupu bird
lays eggs within a termite nest. Each species
works to help the other live. Sometimes,
through dying comes new life...

Our small boat hesitates, is stalled.
A fallen trunk has blocked our waterway.
We must accept an ending and turn back
to find another route.
So different vistas lie ahead,
not those we'd planned, but also
offering delights.
Yet still that pang,
when I look up to watch
the two macaws fly off together.

The comfort of the familiar

By now the jungle haunts our nights.
Rampant vines coil
menacing towards us,
tall trees loom overhead,
and lush green grasses
stretch out to clog
the narrow waterways
our tiny boat threads through.

This is a place of hidden dangers:
flesh-eating ants wait victims,
the anaconda writhes its coils,
darting head of a young boa
scents the air towards us.
We move among these perils fearfully,
knowing we are the aliens,
intruding.
In village settlements blank faces
turn incuriously towards us.
Do they too recognise our otherness?

But then I see, high up above,
a wire that carries power
from one thatched roof to next.
And strung across it, unexpected,
a pair of sand shoes, symbol
of rebellious youth – and recollect
that same scene in my own
suburban street at home,
suddenly aware that,
here, across these thousand miles,
from jungle village to my city home,
there are familiar patterns.
So, after all,
we are a part of one vast world
where interlocking parts
create a jigsaw whole.

Piranha fishing in the Amazon

Stuff of nightmares.
Jagged teeth.
Vicious, menacing.
See pictures of piranhas
tearing unwary flesh,
leaving only whitened bones.
A standard metaphor
for merciless attack.

Around our boat
a darkening night.
Stray jungle sounds.
Black water laps
between the looming trees
where we are moored.

A bite.
A flash of orange
and my baited hook
is seized by predatory jaws.
It's gone.
Again we set the line.
Each time, with cunning,
bait's devoured.
Line goes slack.

At last, a catch.
So small (disarmingly)
this brightly coloured fish,
for such a reputation.
Until prised open mouth
awaits the camera's eye.
I shudder at that vicious jaw,
its armoury of razor teeth.

That night, on board the ship,
the chef has set a platter for us,
piranhas we have caught.
Such irony appeals:
tonight the natural order
is reversed. For now,
no longer prey but predator,
I eat piranha!

Of llamas and piranhas

High in the Andes,
where sprawling grasslands
quilt the earth within surrounding
jagged snow-capped peaks,
herds of llamas roam.
Foolish fond soft muzzles
blunt beneath their long-lashed eyes
and gentle gaze,
running with ungainly grace.

Deep in the Amazon,
in threatening shrouded waterways,
shoals of piranha lurk.
Jagged teeth are razor-sharp
in predatory mouths,
needing the lure of blood,
primed to strip the flesh
from agonizing bones,
bodies a swift flash of orange
through ominous waters.

In mountain fields, patient llamas wait,
beasts of burden,
ready to give meat and wool,
providing for today as forebears
did for Incan lords.

In deep black jungle streams
piranhas just as patient
wait their prey.

Yet llamas spit…

And who knows? Possibly
piranhas love their young?

Ecuador

In the iguana park

In Guayaquil, we found
the famous Iguana Park,
where prehistoric looking creatures
wandered unperturbed
among the feet of marvelling tourists.

Their hooded eyes, watchful,
malevolent, the sickly orange
of their leather skins,
the jagged frill that tapered down
each scaly back, while vicious taloned
claws pad-padded through the crowds.

Monstrous. Evil.

Yet pigeons played among them
unperturbed.
'Another symbiosis,' said the guide.
'The pigeons clean the leather skins
by feeding on that surface.'

So is this intricate world
of Nature's give and take
another lesson for us all?

Walking with tortoises: Galápagos

These giant creatures,
remnants of another world,
ponderous, slow,
leather necks extending,
or hunkered down inside
the monstrous armour of their shells,
remind us what a passing moment
is our life.

Galápagos. The tortoise.
The name they gave the islands.
These are the owners of the place.
We the permitted guests.

So as we tread with care along the path
we see ahead a stately battleship,
full-armoured,
progress deliberately towards us,
unconcerned that we are in its way.
We move aside to let it pass.

And if we hadn't moved? I ask.
Am told he would have come his way,
pushed me aside, just as past campers,
unwary, on a tortoise trail,
have had tents trampled flat.

One must admire such goal-directedness.

But then, I have known people
similarly willing, with no malice,
to forge ahead and lay all low,
that might impede their paths.

Life with birds

At Punta Pitt we climbed the steep rock path,
marvelling at birds we'd never known.
The blue foot boobies and the red,
guarding their nests, indifferent
to our progress, shifting more firmly
two pale blue eggs within each nest.
The male bird, gatherer of twigs,
The female, architect and builder.
Roles defined, but taking care of eggs
and chicks as shared responsibility.

We watched one swoop towards the nest,
precise flight path and landing,
but close behind her came a frigate bird,
the pirate bird, marauder, thief,
ready to steal her catch,

his hooked beak made for sudden theft.
He chased her to the nest, uncaring
that her chicks were waiting,
and snatched her catch away.
Reminder that rapacious greed
is not restricted to our kind.

On Espanola Island

The walk was hard, from rock to rock,
poised perilously, upward, onward,
trying to keep balance as we climbed.

Passing so many wonders:
the dragon lizards, ruffs extended,
reddish-hued, bright eyes fixed on us,
unafraid. Albatrosses guarding eggs,
careful, shifting them, protection
from ground parasites, watch us pass.
Small birds hop close, and little lizards
scurry near our feet.

Until we reach our destination:
a mighty blowhole, where plumes
of water spurt with force towards
the waiting sky. A terrifying sight.
An old volcanic fury now released.

We stand, awestruck, counting waves,
waiting the forthcoming blast.
Such power unleashed, untameable.

Yet in the foreground, lazily at play,
unfazed by spume and spray,
two young seals slide and slither
in the blasts. Reminder that
this is indeed their world,
not ours.

At El Rancho Manzanella

Turtle or tortoise?
Today we leave Galápagos,
the question asked so many times
with different answers, finally resolved.
In English, web foot turtles swim
while tortoises, land creatures,
only float. In Spanish,
one word covers all.

Here in this ranch, where, massive,
ponderous, these ancient creatures
wander free, we ask their age.
No certainties. This one, they guess,
is eighty, may live another sixty years.
A younger one, a stripling, only twenty.
How to tell? The guide points
to the huge and convex dome,
smooth and burnished in the morning sun.
'This one is old.' The younger,
whose striated shell, like wrinkles, is the clue.

Not fair, I think.
Why could not I, also,
find that my skin smooths magically
as I age, instead of adding
these unwanted lines?

The tortoise turns his aged shrewd eyes
towards me, unconcerned.
Or is that sympathy I see?

Transit

Homeward bound

Again in flight, but this time
westward bound. Time to recall,
to juxtapose the fragments of these days,
to find a new perspective,
shift the kaleidoscope,
this way and that.

What was it like?
Always that question,
always awareness that no answer
will be adequate.

I see again the rushing cataracts
of the Iguassu Falls, the pairs
of bright macaws rising, hovering,
above the Amazonian waterways.
I hear the strains of tango music
in the night, as Argentina sways
across my mind, together with
the whispers of the ghosts who walk
La Recoleta, city of the dead.
The bright paint of the Valparaiso houses
glints in the morning Chilean sun;
a mesh of wires for stolen power
in Rio's dense *favela* streets makes mock
of luxury in tourist beaches in Brazil.

Placid dark faces underneath broad hats
above flamboyant garments
of Mamas in Peru, and flocks of llamas
on Andean hills, have served to humanise
the awesome other worldliness
of Machu Picchu's rearing terraces of stone.
Here Incan rulers watched their golden lives
destroyed by Spanish greed for conquest.

Lake Titicaca's reed bed islands, a way of life,
so alien from any I have known,
provides a challenge in its self-containment,
restores a longing for simplicity.
Yet how to balance dense encroaching darkness
of jungles of the Amazon with that
wild freedom of Galápagos, where seabirds wheel
and ancient tortoises watch ages come and go
with shrewd and speculating wisdom in their eyes?

And we who, like conquistadors, have plundered,
taken from this land what we could gain,
can only, like stout Cortés on his peak in Darien,
stand silent, gathering our memories of gold.

Endings

So now we pay the price.

We find we lived on borrowed time.
The day that we had gained
in eastward travel,
racing the sun, like gods,
above the Lilliputian earth,
was ours on loan.
The time has come for debt repayment.

No choices here, for we
are catapulted through the calendar.
Adjust our phones and watches,
accept the missing day
with no regrets –
for what we have been given
has been a time of richness
which, like life itself,
(this also borrowed time)
demands our gratitude,
our willingness to move ahead,
in faith,
accepting golden sunsets,
and the dying of the day.

www.ingramcontent.com/pod-product-compliance
Lightning Source LLC
Chambersburg PA
CBHW072206100526
44589CB00015B/2399